BUTCHER'S DOZEN

BLOODY SUNDAY 50TH ANNIVERSARY EDITION

BUTCHER'S DOZEN

THOMAS KINSELLA

PEPPERCANISTER 30

CARCANET POETRY

CONTENTS

~

~

BUTCHER'S DOZEN

from

THE SAVILLE REPORT

~ CHAPTER 5: THE OVERALL ASSESSMENT ~

5.2 The soldiers of Support Company who went into the Bogside did so as the result of an order by Colonel Wilford, which should not have been given ...

5.4 ...(The) soldiers reacted by losing their self-control and firing themselves, forgetting or ignoring their instructions and training and failing to satisfy themselves that they had identified targets posing a threat or causing death or serious injury... Our overall conclusion is that there was a serious and widespread loss of fire discipline among the soldiers of Support Company.

58. THE BLOODY SUNDAY INQUIRY
Principal Conclusions and Overall Assessment

5.5 The firing by soldiers of 1 PARA on Bloody Sunday caused the deaths of 13 people and injury to a similar number, none of whom was posing a threat of causing death or serious injury.

BUTCHER'S DOZEN

(1972)

I went with Anger at my heel
Through Bogside of the bitter zeal
– Jesus pity! – on a day of cold and drizzle and decay.
A month had passed. Yet there remained
A murder smell that stung and stained.
On flats and alleys – over all –
It hung; on battered roof and wall,
On wreck and rubbish scattered thick,
On sullen steps and pitted brick.
And when I came where thirteen died
It shrivelled up my heart. I sighed
And looked about that brutal place
Of rage and terror and disgrace.
Then my moistened lips grew dry.
I had heard an answering sigh!
There in a ghostly pool of blood
A crumpled phantom hugged the mud:
'Once there lived a hooligan.
A pig came up, and away he ran.
Here lies one in blood and bones,
Who lost his life for throwing stones.'
More voices rose. I turned and saw
Three corpses forming, red and raw,
From dirt and stone. Each upturned face

Stared unseeing from its place:
'Behind this barrier, blighters three,
We scrambled back and made to flee.
The guns cried Stop, and here lie we.'
Then from left and right they came,
More mangled corpses, bleeding, lame,
Holding their wounds. They chose their ground,
Ghost by ghost, without a sound,
And one stepped forward, soiled and white:
'A bomber I. I travelled light –
Four pounds of nails and gelignite
About my person, hid so well
They seemed to vanish where I fell.
When the bullets stopped my breath
A doctor sought the cause of death.
He upped my shirt, undid my fly,
Twice he moved my limbs awry,
And noticed nothing. By and by
A soldier, with his sharper eye,
Beheld the four elusive rockets
Stuffed in my coat and trouser pockets.
Yes, they must be strict with us,
Even in death so treacherous!'
He faded, and another said:
'We three met close when we were dead.
Into an armoured car they piled us
Where our mingled blood defiled us,

Certain, if not dead before,
To suffocate upon the floor.
Careful bullets in the back
Stopped our terrorist attack,
And so three dangerous lives are done –
Judged, condemned and shamed in one.'
That spectre faded in his turn.
A harsher stirred, and spoke in scorn:
'The shame is theirs, in word and deed,
Who prate of Justice, practise greed,
And act in ignorant fury – then,
Officers and gentlemen,
Send to their Courts for the Most High
To tell us did we really die.
Does it need recourse to law
To tell ten thousand what they saw?
The news is out. The troops were kind.
Impartial justice has to find
We'd be alive and well today
If we had let them have their way.
But friend and stranger, bride and brother,
Son and sister, father, mother,
All not blinded by your smoke,
Photographers who caught your stroke,
The priests that blessed our bodies, spoke
And wagged our blood in the world's face.
The truth will out, to your disgrace.'

He flushed and faded. Pale and grim,
A joking spectre followed him:
'Take a bunch of stunted shoots,
A tangle of transplanted roots,
Ropes and rifles, feathered nests,
Some dried colonial interests,
A hard unnatural union grown
In a bed of blood and bone,
Tongue of serpent, gut of hog
Spiced with spleen of underdog.
Stir in, with oaths of loyalty,
Sectarian supremacy,
And heat, to make a proper botch,
In a bouillon of bitter Scotch.
Last, the choice ingredient: you.
Now, to crown your Irish stew,
Boil it over, make a mess.
A most imperial success!'
He capered weakly, racked with pain,
His dead hair plastered in the rain:
The group was silent once again.
It seemed the moment to explain
That sympathetic politicians
Say our violent traditions,
Backward looks and bitterness
Keep us in this dire distress.
We must forget, and look ahead,

Nurse the living, not the dead.
My words died out. A phantom said:
'Here lies one who breathed his last
Firmly reminded of the past.
A trooper did it, on one knee,
In tones of brute authority.'
That harsher spirit, who before
Had flushed with anger, spoke once more:
'Simple lessons cut most deep.
This lesson in our hearts we keep:
You condescend to hear us speak
Only when we slap your cheek.
And yet we lack the last technique:
We rap for order with a gun,
The issues simplify to one –
Then your Democracy insists
You mustn't talk with terrorists.
White and yellow, black and blue,
Have learned their history from you:
Divide and ruin, muddle through.
We speak in wounds. Behold this mess.
My curse upon your politesse.'
Another ghost stood forth, and wet
Dead lips that had not spoken yet:
'My curse on the cunning and the bland,
On gentlemen who loot a land

They do not care to understand;
Who keep the natives on their paws
With ready lash and rotten laws;
Then if the beasts erupt in rage
Give them a slightly larger cage
And, in scorn and fear combined,
Turn them against their own kind.
The game runs out of room at last,
A people rises from its past,
The going gets unduly tough
And you have, surely, had enough.
The time has come to yield your place
With condescending show of grace
– An Empire-builder handing on.
We reap the ruin when you've gone,
All your errors heaped behind you:
Promises that do not bind you,
Hopes in conflict, cramped commissions,
Faiths exploited, and traditions.'
Bloody sputum filled his throat.
He stopped and coughed to clear it out,
And finished, with his eyes a-glow:
'You came, you saw, you conquered…So.
You gorged – and it was time to go.
Good riddance. We'd forget – released –
But for the rubbish of your feast,
The slops and scraps that fell to earth

And sprang to arms in dragon birth.
Sashed and bowler-hatted, glum
Apprentices of fife and drum,
High and dry, abandoned guards
Of dismal streets and empty yards,
Drilled at the codeword "True Religion"
To strut and mutter like a pigeon
"Not An Inch – Up The Queen";
Who use their walls like a latrine
For scribbled magic – at their call,
Straight from the nearest music-hall,
Pope and Devil intertwine,
Two cardboard kings appear, and join
In one more battle by the Boyne!
Who could love them? God above…'
'Yet pity is akin to love,'
The thirteenth corpse beside him said,
Smiling in its bloody head,
'And though there's reason for alarm
In dourness and a lack of charm
Their cursed plight calls out for patience.
They, even they, with other nations
Have a place, if we can find it.
Love our changeling! Guard and mind it.
Doomed from birth, a cursed heir,
Theirs is the hardest lot to bear,
Yet not impossible, I swear,

If England would but clear the air
And brood at home on her disgrace
– Everything to its own place.
Face their walls of dole and fear
And be of reasonable cheer.
Good men every day inherit
Father's foulness with the spirit,
Purge the filth and do not stir it.
Let them out. At least let in
A breath or two of oxygen,
So they may settle down for good
And mix themselves in the common blood.
We all are what we are, and that
Is mongrel pure. What nation's not
Where any stranger hung his hat
And seized a lover where she sat?'
He ceased and faded. Zephyr blew
And all the others faded too.
I stood like a ghost. My fingers strayed
Along the fatal barricade.
The gentle rainfall drifting down
Over Colmcille's town
Could not refresh, only distil
In silent grief from hill to hill.

BLOODY SUNDAY

from
PM DAVID CAMERON'S
PARLIAMENT STATEMENT
15 JUNE 2010

BLOODY SUNDAY

[...] The conclusions of the Report are absolutely clear. There is no doubt, there is nothing equivocal, there are no ambiguities. What happened on Bloody Sunday was both unjustified and unjustifiable. It was wrong...

Lord Saville concludes that the soldiers of the Support Company who went into the Bogside did so as a result of an order which should not have been given by their commander.

He finds that the Support Company reacted by losing their self-control, forgetting or ignoring their instructions and training and with a serious and widespread loss of fire discipline... He finds that, on balance, the first shot in the vicinity of the march was fired by the British Army.

He finds that none of the casualties shot by the soldiers of Support Company was armed with a firearm.

He finds that there was some firing by Republican paramilitaries but none of this firing provided any justification for the shooting of civilian casualties...

And he finds that many of the soldiers – and I quote knowingly – put forward false accounts to seek to justify their firing.

Lord Saville says that some of those killed were clearly fleeing or going to the assistance of others who were dying.

The Report refers to one person who was shot while crawling away from the soldiers. Another was shot in all probability while he was lying mortally wounded on the ground... the Report refers to the father who was hit and injured by army gunfire after going to attend to his son...

Mr Speaker, these are shocking conclusions to read and shocking words to have to say. But, Mr Speaker, you do not defend the British Army by defending the indefensible... What happened should never, ever, have happened...

The government is ultimately responsible for the conduct of the army forces and for that, on behalf of the government, indeed on behalf of our country, I am deeply sorry...

Mr Speaker, the Report also specifically deals with the actions of key individuals in the Army, in politics and beyond, including Major-General Ford, Brigadier McLellan and Lieutenant Colonel Wilford...

In each case the findings are clear. It does the same for Martin McGuinness. It specifically finds he was present and probably armed with a sub-machine gun but it concludes, and I quote - 'we're sure that he did not engage in any activity that provided any of the soldiers with any justification for opening fire.'

I would also like to acknowledge the grief of the families of those killed. They have pursued their long campaign over thirty eight years with great patience. Nothing can bring back those who were killed but i hope, as one relative put it, the truth coming out can help set people free... It is right to pursue the truth with vigour and thoroughness but let me reassure the House there will be no more open-ended and costly inquiries into the past.

THOMAS KINSELLA
~ NOTE ON THE POEM ~

NOTE ON THE POEM

Butcher's Dozen was not written in response to the shooting of the thirteen dead in Derry. There are too many dead on all sides.

The poem was written in response to the Report of the Widgery Tribunal. In Lord Widgery's cold putting aside of truth, the nth in a historic series of expedient falsehoods – with prejudice literally wigged out as Justice – it was evident that we were suddenly very close to the operations of the evil real causes.

I couldn't write the same poem now. The pressures were special, the insult strongly felt and the timing vital if the response was to matter, in all its kinetic impurity. Reaching for the nearest aid I found the aisling – that never quite extinct Irish political verse form – in a late, parodied guise, in the coarse energies and nightmare Tribunal of Merriman's Midnight Court. One changed one's standards, chose the doggerel route, and charged...

The poem was finished, printed and published within a week of the publication of the Widgery Report, and it had the immediate effect I wanted. A regrettable longer term effect has been the loss of friendships and the rejection of my work by English readers.

First published in Great Britain in 2022 by
Carcanet
Alliance House, 30 Cross Street
Manchester, M2 7AQ
www.carcanet.co.uk

A CIP catalogue record for this book is
available from the British Library.

ISBN 978 1 80017 165 7

Book design by Andrew Latimer
Printed in Great Britain by SRP Ltd, Exeter, Devon

The publisher acknowledges financial
assistance from Arts Council England.